Original title:
The Lost Realm

Copyright © 2024 Creative Arts Management OÜ
All rights reserved.

Author: Zachary Prescott
ISBN HARDBACK: 978-9916-90-072-7
ISBN PAPERBACK: 978-9916-90-073-4

Fables of the Unremembered

In shadows deep where whispers dwell,
The tales of time are hard to tell.
Forgotten dreams that softly fade,
In silent woods, they lie betrayed.

Beneath the stars, the stories wake,
Of hearts once bold, now prone to ache.
With every breath, they softly sigh,
Unseen, yet near, they never die.

The Threadbare Map of Yesteryear

A map unfolds, with edges torn,
It speaks of dreams, of hopes reborn.
With faded ink, the paths are drawn,
To places lost, where light has shone.

Each mark a tale of joy or woe,
Where footsteps walked so long ago.
The compass spins, yet finds no truth,
In every line, whispers of youth.

Unseen Bridges to Nowhere

Between the realms of lost and found,
Unseen bridges stretch all around.
They beckon softly, with gentle grace,
To places veiled, an empty space.

Footsteps echo on paths of air,
With dreams unspoken, laid bare.
In shadows rich, they intertwine,
A dance of fate, where souls align.

The Conclave of Wandering Spirits

In moonlit glades, a gathering waits,
Wandering spirits share their fates.
With flickering lights, they gently sway,
In whispers soft, they find their way.

Each tale unfolds like autumn leaves,
Of love once found and hope that grieves.
They gather close, in silent song,
Reminding us where we belong.

Threads of Hope in the Gloom

In shadows deep, where whispers hide,
A flicker glows, a light inside.
Through tangled paths, our spirits weave,
Threads of hope are what we believe.

Each dawn brings warmth to frozen skies,
A tapestry where courage lies.
In darkest nights, we find a seam,
We sew our fears into a dream.

The Ruins of Dreams Half-remembered

In crumbling walls of yesteryears,
Echoes linger, whispering fears.
Fragments scattered, stories blurred,
Lost in silence, barely heard.

The ghosts of wishes, softly sigh,
Painted skies that fade and die.
We gather pieces, patch the past,
In every shard, our dreams are cast.

Sails Adrift in a Starlit Sea

Under the stars, a ship does float,
Waves embrace, a gentle coat.
With tattered sails, we journey wide,
In starlit nights, our dreams abide.

The moon reflects on waters deep,
Guiding paths where shadows creep.
With every breeze, we chase the gleam,
Adrift on tides of whispered dreams.

The Forgotten Pulse of an Old Heart

In rusted clocks, time stands still,
Memories linger, a quiet thrill.
A heart that beats with tales untold,
Whispers of warmth in the bitter cold.

Through tender years and trials faced,
In every echo, love embraced.
The pulse remains, though shadows fall,
A rhythm soft, a fading call.

The Last Breath of Lost Legends

In shadows long past, they tread,
Whispers of glory, now dead.
Heroes once roamed, bold and bright,
Fading like stars into the night.

Forgotten tales under the stone,
Echoes of laughter, now lone.
Each story a flicker, a flame,
Lost in the whispers, yet still remain.

Once they stood tall, hearts ablaze,
Now only shadows in a haze.
Legends that time could not tether,
Interwoven with the forever.

In silence they rest, memories linger,
Each sigh a dance, a ghostly singer.
The last breath of stories once told,
In the hearts of the young and the old.

Haiku of Vanished Echoes

Leaves fall in silence,
Whispers of the past float by,
Echoes lost to time.

Footsteps fade away,
Traces of what once had been,
Nature's soft lament.

Voices in the wind,
Carried through the autumn dusk,
Memories of warmth.

Gentle sighs of air,
Holding secrets, soft and clear,
Life's fleeting embrace.

The Tides of Forgotten Memories

Waves crash on the shore,
Bringing whispers from the deep.
Memories like sand,
Slipping through our fingers, steep.

Ebbing with the moon's pull,
Yearning for moments long gone.
We gaze at the horizon,
Searching for what we've drawn.

Footprints washed away,
By the tides that never sleep.
In the heart of the sea,
Lies the love we wish to keep.

Time keeps flowing on,
Each wave a fleeting embrace,
Carrying our dreams,
Into the depths of space.

A Whisper in the Gathered Gloom

In the shadows' embrace,
Soft whispers weave through the air.
Secrets lost in dusk,
Carried on currents of care.

Night cloaks the world slow,
Darkness, a shroud, bittersweet.
Every breath a sigh,
As echoes of silence meet.

Stars blink in the black,
Guiding the lost through the night.
A flicker of hope,
In the tapestry of fright.

Through the quiet veil,
A voice calls out, gentle, kind.
With each warmth around,
The light begins to unwind.

Legends That Breathe in Silence

In shadows deep, the whispers weave,
Tales of those who dare believe.
Mountains speak of ancient might,
Guardians of the cloaked night.

In stillness, echoes of the past,
Stories that forever last.
Voices carried by the breeze,
Resounding through the ancient trees.

Forgotten paths that intertwine,
Silent oaths, a hidden sign.
In every salt-sprayed wave's embrace,
Legends held in nature's grace.

Beneath the stars, the secrets glow,
Flickering lights that softly show.
In the hush of twilight's breath,
The living pulse of whispered death.

The Traces of Ancient Whispers

In every stone, a story hides,
The echoes of time, where memory bides.
Ancient tongues in the dusk do call,
Shadows of giants, standing tall.

Fragments left on weathered shores,
Soft murmurs of forgotten lore.
In the wind, a soft refrain,
Carrying tales of joy and pain.

Underneath the moon's watchful gaze,
Lies the sweet scent of bygone days.
Whispers twine with the rustling leaves,
Revealing truths that the heart believes.

In the quiet, a history sings,
Of lost realms and fragile things.
Every whisper a thread to trace,
Binding the past in a silent embrace.

The Pathway to Vanished Lands

Beyond the hills where no one walks,
Lies a route of silent talks.
A faded map held in the soul,
Leading to realms beyond control.

Crimson skies and tempests wild,
Whisper like a dreaming child.
Each step a dance on bygone sand,
Guided by fate's unseen hand.

Through twilight mists, the journey weaves,
Crafting pathways, the heart believes.
With every turn, the spirit yearns,
For the lost lands where the fire burns.

And as the stars begin to fade,
In the shadows, truths are laid.
The echoes of adventure call,
In the twilight, we rise or fall.

Timeless Echoes in the Abyss

In depths where light dares not to creep,
Lie the secrets the oceans keep.
Whispers drift like floating dreams,
In the silence, nothing seems.

The abyss holds tales, dark and deep,
Of forgotten souls that never sleep.
Their laughter mingles with the waves,
In the secret heart where silence raves.

Each ripple speaks of ages lost,
A ghostly echo of the cost.
In shadowed currents, memories swim,
Reflected in the ocean's whim.

Time flows like a river's hand,
Drifting softly through this land.
In the stillness of the abyss wide,
Timeless echoes, the forgotten tide.

A Tribute to Lost Lanterns

In the dark, they flickered bright,
Guiding souls through endless night.
Once they glowed with warmth and cheer,
Now their whispers disappear.

Glass and metal, broken dreams,
Fading softly, silent screams.
In the breeze, their voices call,
Echoes of a long-lost hall.

Each flame a story left untold,
Pages turning, gently old.
Yet still we honor what they bore,
Shimmering lights forever more.

The Crossroads of Forgotten Paths

At dusk they meet, the roads aligned,
Where echoes whisper, tales entwined.
Shadows dance beneath the trees,
Carrying the weight of leaves.

Choices linger in the air,
Footsteps tracing dreams laid bare.
Each direction leads to fate,
A story waiting—don't be late.

Faceless wanderers, hearts collide,
In this space where secrets hide.
Paths forgotten, but still alive,
At this crossroads, we survive.

The Unraveling of Timeworn Threads

In the fabric of the years,
Every stitch holds joy and tears.
Timeworn threads begin to fray,
Tales of night and dreams of day.

Gentle hands with wisdom weave,
Patterns that we dare believe.
Yet the loom can stretch and tear,
Lost in moments, caught in air.

Frayed edges of a once-bright cloth,
Whispers of what we were taught.
As we mend, we learn to trust,
From the ashes, rise from dust.

Ghosts in the Garden of Time

Among the blooms, they softly tread,
Hushed voices of the long since dead.
Petals blush with whispered lore,
Secrets held forevermore.

Figures dance in shadows light,
Fleeting glimpses of lost delight.
Every flutter brews a sigh,
In the stillness, dreams can't die.

In this garden, echoes quake,
Memories that we won't forsake.
Time frail, but they remain,
Ghostly whispers, sweet refrain.

Chronicles of the Hidden Land

In a vale where whispers dwell,
Ancient secrets start to swell.
Mountains guard their sacred lore,
Echoes linger evermore.

Roots entwined with tales of old,
In the night, the stars unfold.
Wisdom hidden from the light,
Guides the traveler in the night.

Flowing streams in silence gleam,
Carry dreams on silver beam.
Through the leaves, a story sighs,
Nature's breath beneath the skies.

Each step taken, pathways weave,
In the heart, the souls believe.
Chronicles of a land concealed,
In the silence, truths revealed.

When Time Stood Still

In the hush of morning's glow,
Moments freeze, the world moves slow.
A clock's hands pause in the air,
As if magic holds us there.

Shadows dance with fleeting light,
While the stars remain so bright.
Time entwined in memories,
Where the heart finds gentle ease.

Every glance a story told,
In whispers soft, in glimmers bold.
Lost in dreams where silence reigned,\nA fleeting joy, uncontained.

The sunset blurs from gold to gray,
In this stillness, we shall stay.
When the day has lost its skill,
We embrace the time until.

Echoes of Fading Dreams

In the twilight's gentle sigh,
Whispers of the past float by.
Colors blur, the vision fades,
Memory's dance in soft cascades.

Each step taken, shadows play,
As visions twist and drift away.
Night unveils the tender seams,
Of echoes lost in fading dreams.

Silent wishes on the breeze,
Carried through the ancient trees.
Stars alight with distant songs,
Where every heartbeat still belongs.

In the quiet, we take flight,
Chasing dreams into the night.
Though they scatter like the mist,
In our hearts, they still persist.

Secrets of the Shattered Sky

Beneath the canvas, fractures gleam,
Stars collide in timeless beam.
Whispers weave through cosmic threads,
In silence where our longing spreads.

Clouds of mystery drift above,
Holding tales that we all love.
Fragments bright, a celestial show,
Secrets breathe in twilight's glow.

Earth below and heavens wide,
In the quiet, worlds collide.
From the chaos, dreams arise,
Within the shattered, beauty lies.

Twilight fades, the night awakes,
A dance of fate, as silence shakes.
Secrets linger, softly sigh,
In the echoes of the sky.

Whispers in the Starlit Grove

Beneath the moon's soft glow at night,
Whispers dance in the silver light,
Trees sway gently, secrets unfold,
Every shadow a story told.

Crickets sing a tune so sweet,
Nature's symphony can't be beat,
In the grove where dreams take flight,
Hearts find peace in the still of night.

The Enchanted Veil of Memories

In the mist, where echoes play,
Memories rise like the break of day,
Soft and warm like a lover's touch,
Whispered tales, we cherish much.

Through the veil, we wander slow,
Lost in moments, ebb and flow,
Each smile holds a glimpse of grace,
Time bends here, a tender space.

Paths Worn by Lost Souls

Footsteps fade on dusty trails,
Whispers linger as silence hails,
Each path tells of dreams once grand,
Stories etched in the shifting sand.

Worn and weary, spirits roam,
Searching for a place called home,
In the twilight, shadows blend,
Journeys end where time can mend.

The Return of Silent Lullabies

In the hush of the evening glow,
Lullabies stir, soft and low,
Gentle notes caress the mind,
Carrying dreams, sweetly entwined.

As the stars begin to weep,
Promises drift into our sleep,
Silent songs cradle the night,
Bringing solace until first light.

Requiem for the Unseen Garden

In shadows deep where whispers sigh,
The petals fade, the dreams do fly.
Each leaf a tale of silent grace,
In twilight's hand, an empty space.

Upon the ground, the echoes tread,
Of blossoms lost, of hopes now dead.
The twilight hums a mournful tune,
Beneath the light of the waning moon.

Yet in the dark, a seed remains,
A flicker wrapped in hidden chains.
Awaiting rain, the silent cry,
For life anew, beneath the sky.

So let us weep for what has gone,
In every heart, a quiet dawn.
For gardens unseen still hold their dreams,
In golden light, they weave their seams.

Threads of Time Unraveled

In moments lost, the fabric frays,
We grasp the past in fleeting rays.
Threads of time, both bold and thin,
We weave our stories deep within.

The clockticks echo through the haze,
Capturing dreams in delicate ways.
Each second slips, a transient dance,
Beyond the veil of fate and chance.

In twilight's calm, we stand and gaze,
At tangled fates in a distant maze.
The tapestry of life unwinds,
In every heart, a truth we find.

With every thread, a lesson learned,
Through joy and pain, our spirits turned.
In the loom of night, we find our art,
As threads of time weave from the heart.

Odyssey through the Dreaming Vale

In whispered dreams, the valley calls,
Where twilight shadows gently fall.
Upon the path, the echoes play,
In magic's breath, we drift away.

Through silver mists and starlit streams,
We wander lost in fragile dreams.
Each step a dance, each glance a wish,
In the vale's embrace, the world we miss.

Beneath the boughs, the secrets swell,
In every leaf, a tale to tell.
The laughter mingles with the night,
In the dreaming vale, we find our light.

Awake, we rise as dawn appears,
With cherished hopes, we'll face our fears.
An odyssey carved in heart and soul,
The vale remains, our endless goal.

Beneath the Tattered Banner

United once, now torn away,
Beneath the flag in disarray.
Forgotten dreams in colors fade,
A battle lost in light and shade.

The winds of change, they howl and moan,
Each ripple tells of war and bone.
Yet in the silence, hearts still beat,
In strength of bonds that can't be beat.

We gather 'round the tattered threads,
With stories sung and tears long shed.
For even here beneath the scars,
We lift our gaze towards the stars.

From ashes rise the voices strong,
In hopes that guide us through the wrong.
Beneath the banner, torn but brave,
We stand as one, our spirits save.

A Map of Stars Unseen

In the ink of midnight skies,
Dreams take flight on whispered sighs.
Constellations yet unknown,
Guide the heart where love has grown.

Wander through the dark alone,
Find the paths that lead you home.
Every twinkle, secret spun,
A map of stars, where hope begun.

Silent wishes, softly spoken,
In the vastness, bonds unbroken.
Chasing echoes, lost in beams,
Navigating through the dreams.

Hold the compass in your soul,
Let the starlight make you whole.
When the dawn ignites the sky,
Carry forth the light, oh fly.

Beneath the Weeping Willow

In gentle shade where shadows dance,
Whispers linger, lost in trance.
Beneath the boughs, in soft embrace,
Time slows down, a sacred space.

Leaves like tears fall to the ground,
Stories linger all around.
Memories cradle in the air,
Carried on the breeze of care.

Echoes of the love once shared,
In the silence, hearts prepared.
Roots entwined like lovers' hands,
Strength found where the willow stands.

Listen closely, hear the sighs,
Underneath the painted skies.
In this haven, peace will flow,
Life renews where willows grow.

Labyrinth of Vanished Voices

In corridors of memory's haze,
Whispers linger through the maze.
Footsteps echo, soft and light,
Guiding souls lost in the night.

Secrets fold in shadows deep,
Tales of lost ones never sleep.
Every corner does conceal,
Stories yearning for reveal.

In this labyrinth, silence reigns,
With the pulse of ancient pains.
Reach with hands and touch the past,
Fleeting moments bound to last.

Let their voices softly chime,
In the spaces out of time.
Through this passage, wisdom flows,
A tapestry of lives, who knows?

The Twilight of Forgotten Kings

In twilight's glow, the ruins stand,
Echoes of a once proud land.
Crumbling towers, tales untold,
Where history's heart beats bold.

Crownless heads and broken thrones,
Whisper tales of past alone.
In their shadows, dreams take flight,
Of battles lost, of souls igniting light.

Gaze upon the fading stars,
Know their struggles, their hidden scars.
Ghostly figures in the dusk,
Remembered dreams, in time's own husk.

From ashes rise what once was known,
Through silence, their legacy grown.
In twilight's arms, their wisdom clings,
Through the ages, the song still sings.

Melodies Beneath the Withered Branches

Whispers of wind through the trees,
A song of fate in gentle pleas,
Withered branches cradle the sound,
Lost in the heart where peace is found.

Echoes of laughter, long gone by,
Dance with shadows beneath the sky,
Melodies linger, sweet and low,
In the twilight, where soft winds flow.

Songs of the past intertwine with dreams,
Painting the world in silvery beams,
As twilight deepens into night,
We find solace in the fading light.

Beneath the boughs, secrets reside,
Stories of love and hearts that cried,
Melodies rustle in the dead leaves,
In the stillness, the world believes.

The Enigma of Unfamiliar Faces

In crowded streets where strangers roam,
Each glance a puzzle, far from home,
Eyes like windows, secrets align,
Unfamiliar faces, intertwine.

A fleeting smile, a moment's grace,
The heart holds tight to the unknown space,
Stories etched on every visage,
A tapestry woven in life's passage.

We walk past shadows, unrecognized,
Lives entwined, yet each disguised,
A silent bond that we may share,
The enigma binding us, rare and fair.

Beneath the surface, are we the same?
In the silence, echoes of a name,
In every stranger, a piece we find,
Connecting threads of the human mind.

Cry from the Caverns of Oblivion

Deep in the caverns, shadows play,
Whispers of dreams fade to gray,
A heart's echo rings through the stone,
Cry from the void, a haunting moan.

Forgotten voices call from afar,
Guided by the light of a distant star,
Lost in the mist of time's cruel hand,
A cry of hope in this barren land.

Each cavern holds tales left unsaid,
Songs of the living, the weary dead,
In the darkness, the spirit's grace,
Yearns for freedom in this cold place.

Yet through the depths, a flicker of light,
Stirs in the echoes of endless night,
For every cry that fades away,
Is a promise born of a brand new day.

Echoes of Stars Long Extinguished

In the velvet sky, remnants gleam,
Whispers of light in a distant dream,
Stars once burning, now cold and pale,
Echoes of stories that tell a tale.

Each glimmer a memory, fading fast,
Time's gentle hand erases the past,
Yet in their silence, a beauty lies,
In echoes of hearts, where longing flies.

Across the cosmos, their light persists,
In the dark, we've learned to coexist,
Stars long extinguished still find a way,
To brighten the night, guide us each day.

So look to the heavens, remember their song,
In the spaces between, where we belong,
For every echo of stars that fade,
Is a testament to dreams we've made.

The Abandoned Echo of Yesterday

In the silence where whispers dwell,
Time unfurls its weary shell.
Memories dance in dust and light,
Fading softly into night.

Footsteps linger on cracked stone,
Fragments of laughter, now overblown.
Ghostly shadows weave and weave,
In the heart where dreams believe.

Windows creak with tales untold,
Of lovers young and spirits old.
Every echo, a haunting sigh,
In the corners, where dreams lie.

Yet in the stillness, hope remains,
Brimming softly through the chains.
The past, a song we can't forget,
In whispered tones, our hearts are set.

Veins of Forgotten Rivers

Winding wildly through the land,
Softly cradled in nature's hand.
Echoes of meadows, lush and green,
Where life once flourished, now unseen.

Banks once bright with laughter's sound,
Now in silence, shadows bound.
Every twist, a story lost,
Still we wander, no matter the cost.

The water flows, but none perceive,
The secrets held, the dreams that weave.
Beneath the surface, the past remains,
In gentle currents, joy and pains.

Yet with each ripple, a chance to see,
The beauty in forgotten spree.
For every river, no matter how small,
Holds the echoes of life's great call.

Shadows Cast by Obsidian Dreams

In a realm where nightmares roam,
Silent whispers guide us home.
Obsidian tales, dark yet bright,
Cloaked in the fabric of the night.

Figures dance in twilight's grace,
Chasing shadows, a fleeting trace.
Each heartbeat, a drum of fate,
In haunted halls, we contemplate.

Reflections bend beneath the moon,
The air is thick with ancient tune.
In the shards of dreams, we find our way,
Through the darkness, to the day.

Yet as dawn breaks the spell we weave,
A glimmer of hope we dare believe.
For shadows linger, but light will gleam,
In the embrace of obsidian dream.

Whispers of the Forgotten Winds

Carried softly through the trees,
A gentle rustle, a quiet breeze.
Secrets shared from ages past,
In the air, their shadows cast.

Leaves remember the songs of old,
Stories of love, both shy and bold.
Every gust, a voice that calls,
Echoing through these ancient halls.

Beneath the sky, the world spins round,
In whispers soft, the lost are found.
Faint echoes rest on phantom trails,
Woven deep in the winds' avails.

As twilight drapes the earth in gold,
Quiet truths begin to unfold.
For in the winds, time's magic bends,
And the heart of the world transcends.

Ancient Guardians at the Edge of Dreams

In shadows deep where secrets sleep,
The guardians stand, their watch to keep.
With eyes like stars that pierce the night,
They whisper truths in fading light.

Through whispered winds, their voices flow,
Guiding the lost, the dreamers' glow.
With hands outstretched, they catch our fears,
And turn them soft as gentle years.

Beneath the moon, in silver threads,
They weave the fates of dreamers' beds.
In realms of thoughts, they dance and play,
Eternal watchmen till break of day.

So dare to dream, let visions soar,
For ancient guardians guard the door.
In realms unseen, they hold the streams,
Of all our hopes, at dreams' extremes.

The Mirage of Untouched Worlds

In distant lands where silence hums,
A phantom call from deep drums comes.
Mirages swirl in golden dust,
Untouched by time, where hearts can trust.

These worlds where whispers gently sway,
Hold secrets lost, a warm bouquet.
Each glimmering light, a story spun,
Of realms alive beneath the sun.

Through emerald fields and azure skies,
The mirage beckons, and hope flies.
In every shadow, dreams reside,
Unraveled by the hearts that guide.

To seek the paths untouched by pain,
Is to unearth what still remains.
With every step, our spirits twirl,
In the embrace of untouched worlds.

The Sighs of Harmonies Unheard

In twilight's glow, soft melodies weave,
Notes of the heart that never leave.
The sighs of dreams float on the breeze,
Echoes of love found in the trees.

With each soft sound, a tale unfolds,
Of whispers shared and secrets told.
Harmonies rise, lost in the night,
Filling the void with pure delight.

Yet many hear not the gentle strains,
As life rushes forth with all its chains.
In silent moments, riches abide,
In the pauses where our souls confide.

So listen close, to the world's soft song,
For in its quiet, we all belong.
In sighs of harmonies yet unheard,
Lies the magic of every word.

Crumbling Towers of Time

In shadows tall, the towers stand,
With crumbling stone by nature's hand.
Each brick a tale of ages past,
Of dreams that flew and yet could last.

Through skies of gray, the echoes call,
The rise and fall, the dance of all.
They watch as moments fade away,
Yet hold the light of yesterday.

With every crack, a memory gleams,
Of laughter shared and tender dreams.
In ruins, beauty finds its place,
A silent grace in time's embrace.

So stand with me, beneath this sky,
Among the towers that dare to sigh.
For in their fall, we learn to climb,
To cherish all in crumbling time.

Lullabies in the Wake of Silence

Whispers float on evening air,
Crickets sing a soothing tune,
Stars blink softly, unaware,
As night embraces the moon.

Gentle dreams begin to weave,
Through the stillness of the night,
Captured hearts, but hard to leave,
In a world of pure delight.

Moments linger, shadows blend,
Soft celestial lullabies,
In this silence, wounds can mend,
Underneath the velvet skies.

Hope is cradled in the dark,
Each breath a tender refrain,
In the stillness, love's a spark,
Lighting up this sweet domain.

The Canvas of Ruined Memories

Brushstrokes of a shattered past,
Painted in hues of despair,
Echoes of the shadow cast,
Lost in dreams that float in air.

Faded colors, whispers fade,
Moments trapped on time's cruel frame,
Silent screams, a masquerade,
All that's left is callous flame.

Fragments of a love once bright,
Etched in shadows on the wall,
Ghostly visions, dimmest light,
In this silence, memories call.

Artistry in broken lines,
Seeking solace in the scars,
Within the hues, the heart still shines,
Beneath the dust of fallen stars.

Journals from the Edge of Oblivion

Pages worn, a tale untold,
In the margins, dreams collide,
Whispers lost in memories old,
Secrets held where shadows bide.

Ink that bleeds with every thought,
Capturing the fleeting flight,
Yearning for the battles fought,
Flickers in the fading light.

Embers glowing, ghosts of fate,
Each entry a bittersweet song,
On the edge, they softly wait,
Navigating what feels wrong.

Where oblivion's breath creeps close,
Words can tether fragile minds,
In the dark, the heart still knows,
Hope in ink, through time it binds.

The Dance of Dust and Shadows

In the twilight, shadows play,
Dusty rays of light embrace,
Fleeting moments fade away,
In a slow and soft ballet.

Whirling with the secrets kept,
Underneath the filtered glow,
Through the silence, spirits leapt,
In the dance of ebb and flow.

Whispers echo off the walls,
Memories in faded hues,
Gentle grace through time installs,
Stories woven in the muse.

And as the night begins to wane,
Dust and shadows twirl and glide,
In their dance, a bittersweet pain,
Where the past and future bide.

Echoes Through a Broken Portal

A whisper through the shattered frame,
Lost voices call my name.
Fragments of a time long gone,
Dancing shadows greet the dawn.

In twilight's glow, they softly weep,
Guarding secrets, buried deep.
The air is thick with tales untold,
Of dreams once bright, now worn and old.

I step inside this fractured space,
To find a memory, to trace.
The echoes guide my trembling heart,
Through realms where dreams and ghosts depart.

As silence falls, the past awakes,
With every sound, the portal shakes.
Yet in this night of whispered lore,
I find a way, to feel once more.

The Veil of Silent Secrets

Beneath the starlit sky's embrace,
Lies a truth we dare not face.
Shadows cling to ancient walls,
Where quiet whispers softly calls.

In the stillness of the night,
Hidden stories take their flight.
Veils of silence guard the past,
In this realm, where shadows cast.

Eyes that flicker with delight,
Holding dreams, lost to the night.
Every secret, tightly wound,
In the silence, they are found.

The air is thick with somber tones,
Each heartbeat shares forgotten moans.
Yet within this hushed expanse,
Lies a chance for a new dance.

Faded Footprints in the Mist

Along the path where shadows linger,
Footprints fade, like a ghostly singer.
Hidden stories in the haze,
Whispering of forgotten days.

Each step steps softly on the ground,
Memories in the mist are found.
Time erodes, but still I seek,
The echoes of the past I speak.

In gentle waves, the fog rolls by,
Hiding dreams that once could fly.
Faded marks in nature's embrace,
Guide me through this timeless space.

Within the silence, I can feel,
The history that won't conceal.
Footprints lead me to the truth,
In whispers soft, I find my youth.

Memories of a Hidden Sanctuary

In a glade where wildflowers bloom,
Lies a haven, free from gloom.
Softly sheltered, nature's grace,
A secret world, a hidden space.

Breezes dance through ancient trees,
Carrying whispers on the breeze.
Sunlight filters, golden light,
Awakening dreams from the night.

Each rustle tells a tale to share,
Of gentle moments, beyond compare.
In this sanctuary, I find rest,
Wrapped in peace, I feel so blessed.

Time stands still in this embrace,
Here, my heart finds its rightful place.
Memories linger, love's sweet song,
In this refuge, I belong.

Whispers of Forgotten Winds

In the heart of the silent glen,
Whispers of tales once told begin,
Carried by breezes soft and thin,
Secrets of lost time linger within.

Leaves tremble in the fading light,
Each rustle speaks of ancient flight,
Echoes of laughter, lost in night,
In the stillness, hope takes flight.

Stars awaken as shadows blend,
Guiding the wanderers, their only friend,
Through paths where memory won't end,
In the dark, all souls transcend.

The night holds wonders yet to find,
In every breeze, the world's entwined,
A tapestry of hearts combined,
Whispers of love forever blind.

Shadows Beneath the Ruins

Beneath the stones where silence dwells,
Shadows weave their secret spells,
Tales of glory, loss, and shouts,
In crumbling walls, the past resounds.

Faded echoes of laughter trace,
Ghostly figures time can't erase,
Footsteps lost in the ancient space,
Whispers linger, a soft embrace.

Moonlight dances on broken floors,
Remnants of dreams behind shut doors,
In every crack, a history pours,
Silent witnesses to life's roars.

As shadows deepen, stories spin,
In the twilight, the journey begins,
Through memories that softly grin,
In ruins where the heart still wins.

Echoes from an Abandoned Throne

Dust settles on the regal seat,
An empty crown, tales bittersweet,
Echoes of power, lost to time,
In loneliness, a silent rhyme.

Glimmers of grandeur fade away,
Once vibrant halls now shadow play,
Whispers of rulers who've had their say,
In moments where dreams drift and sway.

Forgotten voices call from the past,
In every heart, memories cast,
A throne once bold, now overgrown,
In solitude, the soul is sown.

Yet in the stillness, a spark remains,
Hope to reclaim what time disdains,
In shadows deep, the spirit gains,
A dance of echoes, life sustains.

The Veil of Silent Echoes

A gentle shroud envelops the night,
Veiling whispers that take to flight,
Silent echoes weave through the trees,
Carried softly by the night's breeze.

Dreams like shadows flicker and weave,
Stories spun for those who believe,
In the quiet, the heart can see,
Messages whispered from the free.

Stars blink secrets in the dark,
Guiding wanderers to their mark,
With each sigh of the ancient ground,
In silence, lost hopes are found.

The veil hangs thick yet breathes with grace,
In every pause, the world finds space,
For in the silence, all can trace,
A unity of time and place.

The Dance of Invisible Souls

In twilight's veil, they swirl and weave,
Silent whispers that none perceive.
Their laughter lingers, soft and light,
A fleeting dance that haunts the night.

With every step, a story told,
Of moments cherished, of love grown bold.
In shadows deep, their essence glows,
An endless waltz where time bestows.

Through starlit realms, they drift and sway,
A ballet stitched in dreams' array.
Their presence felt, yet never seen,
In every heart, a sacred scene.

Invisible souls, forever bound,
In the silence, their truth is found.
An ageless rhythm, a cosmic tune,
They dance beneath the silver moon.

Wandering Through the Forgotten Woods

In the heart where shadows breathe,
Ancient trees with secrets sheathe.
A whispered path, a tale untold,
Through roots and leaves, the past unfolds.

Mossy stones beneath the sky,
Echoes of those who once passed by.
The brook sings soft, a mirrored dream,
In nature's grasp, all lost may gleam.

Each step reveals a world once known,
Of wanderers, their seeds were sown.
In every hush, a spirit glides,
Through tangled branches where hope abides.

With twilight's brush, the forest glows,
Revealing all that time bestows.
And in the stillness, hear the call,
Of wandering souls, embraced by all.

Tales from the Silent Expanse

Where stars align in velvet black,
Whispers rise from the cosmic track.
Each point of light, a story glows,
In the silence, the universe knows.

Constellations weave the dreams we spin,
A canvas vast, our souls begin.
Galaxies swirl, their secrets bare,
In the quiet night, we pause and stare.

Echoes linger from ages past,
Upon the wind, their voices cast.
Time drifts softly, like dust in air,
Collecting tales beyond compare.

In solitude, the heart takes flight,
Exploring depths of endless night.
The silence sings, a lullaby,
Of all that's seen and all that's nigh.

Echoes of the Unretrieved

In forgotten dreams where shadows play,
Reside the echoes of yesterday.
Memories whisper, soft and low,
In the silence, their essence flows.

Fragments linger, like mist on ground,
Lost in the woods where hope is found.
With each heartbeat, a tale sings clear,
Of all we've known and held so dear.

Time's tapestry, a woven thread,
Holds the whispers of words unsaid.
In the quiet, truths intertwine,
Revealing paths that once were mine.

Yet through the depths, a light will gleam,
In every sorrow, a hidden dream.
The echoes linger, never flee,
In the heart's embrace, they journey free.

Fables Adrift in Mist

Whispers weave through silent woods,
Where shadows tell their ancient tales.
The echo of forgotten broods,
In twilight's trance, the memory pales.

A ghostly figure drifts with grace,
Each crackling leaf a story spun.
In every corner of this place,
The fables dance, the night's begun.

Beneath the fog, the secrets lie,
In tangled roots, in dreams confined.
Where time stands still and spirits sigh,
Fables drift, the myths remind.

A lantern's glow, a fleeting ray,
Guides lost souls through the twisted paths.
As dawn approaches, shades decay,
Yet in the mist, the magic lasts.

Haunting Melodies of a Hidden Place

In the forest where echoes play,
A silent choir sings so sweet.
The branches sway, they dance away,
With every note, our hearts entreat.

A breeze reveals the songs untold,
Whispers of love, and pain, and loss.
The air is thick with tales of old,
Where time forgets its heavy cross.

Each note a wish, each sigh a dream,
Carried softly on the wind's embrace.
In shadows deep, like moonlight's beam,
We lose ourselves in this hidden place.

A melody that knows no end,
It lingers long after we part.
In every heart, it will descend,
A haunting tune that wakes the heart.

The Silent Call of the Abyss

Below the waves where silence reigns,
A call emerges from the deep.
In hidden depths, no words remain,
Yet every secret, there, I keep.

The shadows dance in darkest blue,
Where time and tide forever blend.
A realm where dreams may drift anew,
In depths that stretch, no bounds to lend.

The siren's song, a ghostly plea,
Invites the brave to plunge below.
The silent call pulls heart and glee,
Into the depths where stars don't glow.

And in that void where echoes cease,
I find a solace, calm and pure.
In darkened waves, I feel my peace,
The abyss calls, an endless lure.

Dreams Entwined in Twilight

As dusk descends, our visions blend,
In hues of violet and soft gold.
Where every dream begins to mend,
In twilight's arms, the night unfolds.

The whispered hopes take flight and soar,
Across the sky, in colors bright.
They dance upon the ocean's roar,
And weave through stars, a dazzling sight.

Each fleeting moment captures grace,
In shadows cast by fading light.
With every breath, we find our place,
In dreams entwined, we chase the night.

These visions born, not lost but shared,
In every heart, a longing spark.
As twilight kisses all unprepared,
We drift away, surrendered, dark.

Ephemeral Footsteps on Forgotten Sands

Waves gently kiss the shore's embrace,
Footprints fade in a silent trace.
Moments lost in the ocean's sigh,
Memories linger, beneath the sky.

Time dances lightly on grains of gold,
Stories whispered, yet untold.
Each step a breath, each breath a dream,
Fleeting as sunlight, they silently gleam.

The tide rolls in, its secrets deep,
Eroding pathways, our echoes keep.
Yet in the dunes, life finds a way,
To cradle the past, to welcome the day.

Nature reclaiming what once was ours,
Blending our essence with the stars.
Footsteps fade, but souls will stand,
Eternal whispers on forgotten sand.

The Last Light of a Dying Sun

Crimson spills across the evening sky,
As day bows low with a gentle sigh.
Golden rays slip beneath the hill,
Fading softly, a time to still.

Shadows stretch as whispers grow,
The world embraces twilight's glow.
Stars awaken, in silence they hum,
A serenade for the day that's done.

The horizon blushes, a fleeting kiss,
In this quiet moment, we find our bliss.
With the last light, dreams take their flight,
Holding tightly to the beauty of night.

The sun may set, but hope will rise,
In embered skies, where the spirit flies.
Cherish the dusk, and welcome the dawn,
As time flows on, and the day is gone.

Sunflowers in the Forgotten Fields

Golden faces turn to the sky,
Sturdy stems where whispers lie.
Petals like sunbeams, a vibrant glow,
Guarding secrets of long ago.

Breezes carry tales of old,
In fields of wonder, brave and bold.
Dancing lightly, they sway and bend,
Nature's laughter that will not end.

Each bloom a beacon, bright and warm,
A symbol of hope amidst the storm.
In forgotten corners, they proudly stand,
An ode to beauty, hand in hand.

Though time may weary, they shall remain,
A testament to joy, born from pain.
Their vibrant hearts shall never fade,
In forgotten fields, life's serenade.

Lost Songs of Celestial Meadows

In meadows kissed by starlit grace,
Echoes linger, time can't erase.
Whispers of night weave through the trees,
A symphony sung by the gentle breeze.

Beneath the moon's soft, watchful gaze,
Nature hums in a golden haze.
Flowers sway to a silent tune,
Beneath the watchful eye of the moon.

Lost are the songs of ancient days,
Yet through the stars, their magic plays.
Every flower tells a tale untold,
A secret garden, forever bold.

As morning breaks, the music flows,
From every petal, the melody grows.
In celestial meadows, dreams take flight,
Lost songs awakening in the gentle light.

Beneath the Ashen Skies

Under the shroud of gray, they weep,
Whispers carried on the wind, they creep.
Faint embers glow where shadows lie,
Lost dreams linger, beneath ashen sky.

The world, a canvas of muted tones,
Echoes of laughter, now just moans.
In the silence, hope seems to wane,
Yet within the heart, a flicker remains.

Fallen leaves dance in the bitter breeze,
Stories untold float through the trees.
Beneath the weight of a brooding cloud,
A spark of defiance stands unbowed.

With heavy hearts, we trace our fate,
Beneath the ashen skies, we wait.
For in the dusk, a dawn may rise,
And from the ashes, a new surprise.

Secrets Beneath the Ancient Stone

In shadows deep where secrets lie,
Ancient stones breathe a hidden sigh.
Carved by time, their stories stay,
Guardians of dreams lost along the way.

The whispers of ages, soft and low,
Invoke the past in their gentle flow.
Each crack and crevice, a tale obscure,
A labyrinth of truths, dark yet pure.

Beneath the weight of a timeless crust,
Echoes of wisdom blend with dust.
In silence, the ancient voices sing,
Revealing the beauty that memories bring.

We kneel before the history's throne,
Awed by the secrets beneath the stone.
For in the heart of the earth, we find,
A connection that binds all of mankind.

Lost in the Labyrinth of Time

Twisted paths lead us far and wide,
In the labyrinth of time, we bide.
Moments pass, like whispers in the air,
Finding solace in the maze, so rare.

Echoes of laughter, traces of tears,
Woven together, the fabric of years.
Each corner turned, a choice defined,
In the depths of our heart, our truths aligned.

Chasing shadows that flicker and fade,
In search of the memories, unafraid.
The clock ticks on, relentless in might,
While dreams intertwine with the stars at night.

Though lost at times in the endless chase,
We carry the wisdom, the loving grace.
For every twist in the passage of rhyme,
Leads us closer to the heart of time.

Twilight over the Sunken City

At dusk the waters gently sigh,
Beneath the waves, the tales lie.
Sunken dreams in a world of blue,
Whispers of life that once flourished anew.

The ruins rise from the ocean's deep,
Guardians of memories, secrets to keep.
In twilight's glow, they shimmer with grace,
A haunting reminder of an ancient place.

Stars begin to flicker in the night,
Casting shadows with a silver light.
Stories unfold beneath the tide,
In the embrace of the waves, dreams abide.

As the moon drapes her veil of glow,
The sunken city tells tales of woe.
Yet in the twilight, hope's embers burn,
In the depths of the sea, we yearn, we learn.

Remnants of a Stolen Age

Whispers of the past remain,
Echoes in the silent night.
Shadows dance upon the ground,
Memories of lost delight.

Crumbled walls and dusty stones,
Tell tales of an ancient plight.
Voices lost in time's embrace,
Fading fast from mortal sight.

Ghostly figures drift about,
Haunting dreams of what once was.
In the ruins, stories weave,
Tales of love and broken laws.

Yet in silence, hope still glows,
Through the dark, a faint reprise.
Remnants hold the strength of time,
Beneath the weight of endless skies.

The Journey to Nowhere

Steps that trace a timeless path,
Lead us through the endless night.
Wandering souls in search of truth,
Always striving for the light.

Roads entwined with sorrow's thread,
Every mile a tale unfolds.
In the stillness, questions rise,
What is found, what is sold?

Branches stretch toward a void,
Where dreams meet the edge of fate.
Travelers lost in their own minds,
As the dawn begins to wait.

Yet each step ignites the fire,
Of a heart that dares to seek.
In the rhythm of the night,
Lives the voice that whispers, "Speak."

Fragments of a Shattered World

Broken glass underfoot lies,
Each shard tells a secret tale.
In the chaos, beauty hides,
Waiting for the brave to sail.

Winds that carry whispers soft,
Brush through ruins and decay.
In the fragments, hope still breathes,
Guiding hearts that have lost their way.

Pictures painted with despair,
Faded colors, lifeless hue.
Yet within the cracked embrace,
Lives a spark of something new.

Together, we rebuild the dreams,
From the ashes, rise we must.
In the shards, a future gleams,
A promise forged from love and trust.

In the Grip of Unseen Forces

Threads of fate spin round and round,
Binding all in hidden ways.
In the shadows, hands reach out,
Guiding paths through endless maze.

Whispers ride the breath of night,
Carrying secrets yet untold.
In the grip of unseen sway,
Life's true rhythm, brave and bold.

Dancing lightly on the edge,
Of dreams forged in silver light.
We are but marionettes here,
Pulled by strings both soft and tight.

Still we seek to break the chains,
Yearning for a strength to soar.
In the grip, we find our voice,
A melody forevermore.

Visions of a World Unclaimed

Beyond the hills where silence grows,
Whispers of dreams in twilight flows.
A canvas vast, unmarked by time,
Echoes of love in every rhyme.

Beneath the stars, the night awakens,
Paths untraveled, yet heart is shaken.
Wonders wait in the gentle breeze,
Endless tales beneath the trees.

Colors dance in the morning light,
Nature's song reveals pure delight.
A world untouched by human hands,
Where peace and harmony still stands.

In every shadow, a story lies,
Promises held in the vast blue skies.
Visions bloom where hope remains,
A world unclaimed, love's eternal gains.

A Heartbeat Beneath the Dust

In ruins old, time softly breathes,
A ghostly hum that never leaves.
Whispers trapped in faded stones,
Echo the lives that once called home.

Beneath the dust, a rhythm flows,
Stories of love, fears, and woes.
Each heartbeat lost in silent night,
Longing for dawn, for a guiding light.

Echoes of laughter, shadows cast,
Memories held from a distant past.
The heartbeat pulses, steady, true,
Reminding us of what once grew.

From ashes rise the dreams anew,
In every crack, life breaks through.
A heartbeat strong where hope reigns vast,
In the silence, the present meets the past.

Legends Carved in Shadows

In every shadow, stories weave,
Tales of heroes who dared to believe.
Carved in night where whispers dwell,
Echoes of legends, a timeless spell.

Beneath the moon, the ancients call,
Their voices strong, their shadows tall.
Wisdom shared in the soft night air,
Memories linger, beyond despair.

Each step we take, their ghosts inspire,
A flickering flame, a burning fire.
Legends told by the flickering light,
Guide our paths through the darkest night.

In twilight's glow, we seek the truth,
Holding tight to our lost youth.
With every heartbeat, the stories rise,
Legends last beneath the skies.

Remnants of a Forgotten Age

Where time stands still, the echoes fade,
Remnants left of a grand parade.
Fragments of laughter, whispers of time,
Ancient memories in soft rhyme.

Worn paths speak of tales once shared,
In silent woods, the spirits bared.
Lost wonders hide in shadows deep,
Promises made that time will keep.

Dusty tomes filled with a past,
In every page, a tether cast.
Voices linger, soft as a sigh,
In forgotten realms where dreams don't die.

Beneath our feet, the stories hum,
Of distant lands where hearts still drum.
Remnants linger in the fading light,
A forgotten age, yet ever bright.

The Ghosts of When We Were

In the whispering echoes of yesterday,
Laughter dances on the wind,
Memories flicker like fading stars,
In the twilight where dreams rescind.

Footsteps trace the path we used,
Through the gardens of our youth,
Every corner holds a moment,
Each shadow tells a truth.

In pictures worn and colors lost,
We find the warmth of what was ours,
Yet time, it steals, it pays its cost,
As we gaze at distant hours.

But still the spirits linger here,
In every laugh, in every tear,
Though seasons change and days grow dim,
The ghosts of when will never swim.

Shimmering Dust in an Eclipsed Light

Stars lie hidden in silent skies,
Wrapped in shadows thick and deep,
Yet glimmers flicker, soft and shy,
Like secrets whispered in our sleep.

Through the veil of muted gleam,
We reach for dreams that softly fade,
In the heart of night, a fleeting beam,
Where hope and fear are gently laid.

Dust of time, it coats the air,
In moments lost, we find our fight,
For in the dark, we dance with care,
Chasing shimmering dust in eclipsed light.

So hold the stars within your palm,
Let the shadows pass us by,
For even in the quiet calm,
The light persistently will lie.

Secrets Beneath the Ruined Arch

Beneath the stones of ancient tales,
Whispers linger in the breeze,
Through cracks and gaps, the memory pales,
And breathes among the withered trees.

A forgotten path, a silent plea,
Hides stories written in the dust,
In every crack is history,
In every shadow, echoes thrust.

The arches stand, though time has wear,
Guardians of a past so bold,
In the silence, secrets share,
Life and love that once were told.

So pause here in this quiet vale,
Let the past unfurl its heart,
For every ruin tells a tale,
And every end is a new start.

The Melancholy of Shadowed Places

In the corners where the light recedes,
Lies a weight too deep to bear,
The sigh of dreams that once took seed,
Now tangled in the still, cold air.

Every shadow casts a long embrace,
Whispered hopes and silent cries,
In the silence, we find our space,
As the dusk gives way to sighs.

In the depths of forgotten halls,
Ghostly whispers brush the skin,
Echoing through the crumbling walls,
Changing minds and hearts within.

Yet in the melancholy's flow,
There's beauty in the tear-streaked past,
For in the pain, we learn to grow,
And in the darkness, light is cast.

The Lament of Lost Horizons

In twilight's grasp, the dreams decay,
Once bright, now shadows drift away.
The sails of hope, now tattered, torn,
Beneath the weight of worlds forlorn.

The whispers of a distant shore,
Haunt memories we can't restore.
With every step, a haunting groan,
As echoes mark the path we've flown.

A fading sun paints skies in grief,
Where once stood joy, now just belief.
The horizon calls, a siren's wail,
Yet joy remains but a ghostly trail.

So here we stand, at life's cruel bend,
Where lost horizons twist and bend.
In search of light, we still pursue,
A fleeting glimpse of what was true.

The Haunting of Desolate Paths

Upon the road where shadows creep,
The whispers of the past still seep.
Each step I take, a silent scream,
In haunted lands where phantoms dream.

The trees, they bend with unseen weight,
As memories weave a tangled fate.
In empty halls, the voices call,
Their echoes dance within these walls.

Eclipsed by moonlight's ghostly dance,
The siren songs invite a chance.
Yet in the mist, I fear to tread,
For paths like these are lost, not led.

Beneath the stars, the darkened night,
Holds stories veiled, no end in sight.
And though I walk these paths alone,
I'm bound to find what fate has sown.

Wraiths of the Faded Horizon

In azure skies where dreams take flight,
The wraiths emerge at fall of night.
They beckon forth with softest sighs,
A dance of lost and aching cries.

The horizon stretches, blurred and dim,
Where light and shadow twist on whim.
Each fading star a tale untold,
A thread of time, worn down and old.

With chilling winds they roam the land,
Their fingers brushing grains of sand.
And in the silence, stories churn,
The lessons of the past we learn.

Yet through the gloom, a spark remains,
A flicker of hope, despite the chains.
For as the wraiths of night take flight,
They weave the dawn, igniting light.

A Tapestry of Untold Tales

In the loom of life, threads intertwine,
Weaving stories, both yours and mine.
Each strand a whisper, a truth, a fall,
A tapestry born of silence's call.

Upon the fabric, colors blend,
Echoes of journeys that twist and bend.
From joy to sorrow, each hue portrays,
The essence of our fleeting days.

The weaver sits with hands so skilled,
Crafting the tales that fate has thrilled.
In every pattern, a lesson flows,
Of pain and laughter, of love that grows.

So gather round, let stories ignite,
For in this tapestry, we find our light.
With every stitch, a life reclaimed,
In untold tales, we are all named.

The Secret in the Forgotten Glade

In the heart where silence sways,
Ancient trees guard hidden ways.
Soft light filters through the leaves,
Keeping secrets that nature weaves.

A brook sings low, a gentle tune,
Under the gaze of a silver moon.
Each ripple knows the tale it tells,
Of magic wrapped in verdant spells.

Footprints linger, yet not a soul,
Wanders here to feel the whole.
In whispers soft, the glade confides,
Where time itself, in stillness hides.

Nature's breath, a soft decree,
Invites the heart to wander free.
In this secret, lost yet found,
The forgotten glade speaks profound.

Reflections of an Ancient Echo

In caverns deep where shadows dwell,
Ancient echoes weave their spell.
Whispers molded by time's embrace,
Reveal the past in a fleeting trace.

Voices linger in twilight's glow,
Softly urging hearts to know.
Mirror shards of history,
Reflecting life's great mystery.

Each laugh and tear, a story bold,
In echoes learned, a truth unfolds.
Carried forth on time's swift tide,
Ancient tales refuse to hide.

Listen close, the world will share,
All its wisdom, lost and rare.
In every sound, a lesson gleams,
Reflections of forgotten dreams.

Whispers of Forgotten Dreams

In twilight's hush, a secret sigh,
Awakens dreams that long did lie.
Softly woven in the night,
Whispers dance in silver light.

Each fleeting thought, a phantom's grace,
Lingering in a timeless space.
Ghostly echoes of hopes now fade,
Yet shimmer still in the darkened shade.

If you listen, you might hear,
The gentle call of what's held dear.
In every heart, a dream resides,
Yearning still, though time decides.

Breathe in deep, let minds explore,
The realms of dreams that wait, implore.
For in these whispers, truths abide,
Forgotten dreams shall not reside.

Shadows of an Abandoned Kingdom

In crumbled halls where echoes weep,
The shadows linger, memories keep.
Thrones of dust in silence stand,
Guarding tales of a once-great land.

Through broken walls, the winds do sigh,
A mournful song of bygone sky.
Each stone a witness, ancient, wise,
Beneath the watchful, empty skies.

Lost are the voices, their laughter flown,
In withered gardens, seeds un grown.
Yet in the twilight, a warmth remains,
Of love and loss in eternal chains.

Walk softly here, tread with care,
For shadows dance in the cool night air.
Amid the ruins, histories blend,
In the echoes, life will transcend.

Milton Keynes UK
Ingram Content Group UK Ltd.
UKHW022144111124
451073UK00007B/182